Outside
Mullingar

Outside Mullingar

John Patrick Shanley

THEATRE COMMUNICATIONS GROUP
NEW YORK
2014

The publication of *Outside Mullingar*, by John Patrick Shanley, through TCG's Book Program, is made possible in part by the New York State Council on the Arts with the support of Governor Andrew Cuomo and the New York State Legislature.

TCG books are exclusively distributed to the book trade by Consortium Book Sales and Distribution.

LIBRARY OF CONGRESS CATALOGING-IN-PUBLICATION DATA
Shanley, John Patrick.
Outside Mullingar / John Patrick Shanley.
pages cm
ISBN 978-1-55936-475-1 (paperback)
ISBN 978-1-55936-786-8 (ebook)
I. Title.
PS3569.H3337O97   2014
812'.54—dc23   2013050920

Cover, book design and composition by Lisa Govan
Front cover photograph by Todd Heisler/*New York Times*/Redux
Back cover photograph by iStockphoto

First Edition, January 2014

For my family, old and new, Irish and American,
most especially for my sons Nick and Frank

Introduction

My father came from Ireland and he had the gift of the gab. Part of the reason the Irish developed the gift of the gab was simple. They lived on an island. They had to get along. Not that they did get along. But they had to try. So a style of speaking developed that allowed them to say awful things. With charm.

I am not Irish. I am Irish-American. Some say I have the gift as well. If I do, it is because I listened to my father and my uncles and some of my aunts as they gave as good as they got in my living room in the Bronx. On many the Saturday night, they would drink rye and ginger ale, and smoke and talk and sing and dance, and I would sing, too, and dance with my aunts, and listen through the blue air. And because I listened to so much talk and so much music, perhaps I was spared somehow from the truly unfortunate fate of being an uneloquent Irish-American.

My father played a very particular accordion. It had his name spelled out in rhinestones, and emblazoned over his

name, the crossed flags of Ireland and America, also in rhinestones. It was a wedding present from somebody, grandparents
I think. All my grandparents were Irish and had died before
I was born, so they melded in my mind into a kind of mono-
lithic ancient green mush. My father played many Irish songs
on this squeezebox, and Elvis Presley's "Love Me Tender."
When he sang it, it was the most Irish song of all.

When I went to Ireland for the first time, in 1993, I was
forty-two. My father was in his late eighties, and I went with
him to visit the family farm outside the village of Killucan,
near the town of Mullingar, in County Westmeath. I had just
gotten my New York driver's license a few weeks before, and
I was a hideous driver. I had to drive for one hundred miles
on the wrong side of the road. Periodically, my father would
say, "Watch out!" as I was seconds from killing us both. By the
time we got to the farm, I had lost a side mirror and was in a
poor emotional condition.

We turned into the rustic dirt driveway. The farm looked
completely dead. I could see a couple of motionless sheep on
a distant ridge—otherwise, nothing. I rolled my rented car
down to the farmhouse and shut it off. The silence was so com-
plete I could feel it on my skin.

I knocked. The door was opened softly and with caution.
Looking at me was my cousin Anthony. His eyes burned with
a mad blue intensity. He greeted us quietly and in we went.
In the house, which we entered by way of the kitchen, were
stacks of people, all close relations.

No sooner had we cleared the door than all hell broke
loose. My Aunt Mary was sitting by the turf stove, leaning
on a cane. She let fly with a vigorous speech, not one word of
which I could understand, though she was apparently speaking English. Her husband, my Uncle Tony, turned out in a
Greek fishing cap, white shirt and weathered vest, was waving
a pipe. He had electric blue eyes as well, the eyes of a mala-
mute, and a crafty, gleeful expression. He, too, was holding
forth, and although I could not understand a word of what he

was saying either, his accent was utterly different than that of his wife. He spoke in a measured and forceful tone, while Mary's declarations came out at the rate of water gushing from a fire hose.

The one linguistic quality they shared was emphasis. Each and every thing they said was said with an air of such conviction it seemed impossible anyone could disagree. And yet, they did disagree, and attempted to shout down and dismiss every statement made by the other.

Uncle Tony and Aunt Mary weren't the only ones speaking in this small country kitchen, which smelled of brown bread, oatmeal, pipe smoke and turf. Several cousins were present and also speaking. Some were shouting that we must be exhausted, in shock from the severity of our journey, or hungry, or in need of a chair. At least, these ideas were ones I thought I could pick out.

My father watched all this with a serene expression. He had been coming here for many years, in addition to having been born here, and none of this, I suppose, was new to him. It was perhaps ten in the morning. Miraculously, a gap appeared in the conversation, and my cousin Audrey managed to ask if we would like breakfast. My father said he would like a drink of whiskey and sat down.

There was no lighting. That is, there were lights, but not one of them was turned on. One small window let in the few photons that had survived the rain and clouds. These heroic if anemic lumens shouldered the full task of illuminating the kitchen. It was not enough.

Basically, what I was experiencing was a pack of Irish people shouting in the dark.

I sat down by my father in the gloom, refused a drink of my own in favor of tea and oatmeal, and asked if there had been a power failure. This set off a series of denunciations and exhortations about the light switch, which was finally thrown by my cousin Anthony as if he were setting fire to the national treasury or electrocuting the only woman he had ever loved.

When the light came on, Anthony recoiled from its rays. He squinted and dropped his eyes to save his retinas, I suppose, from incineration.

Unfortunately, this tactic caused him fresh disturbance. Because now he cried out in horror that the floor was a disgrace, that it was crusted in muck and alive with dust. I looked at the linoleum floor and saw nothing. He got a broom and began to sweep like a demon, relatives leaping out of his way. I said the floor was perfect as it was. He told me that I was mad, nothing less than unstable and possibly dangerous. I decided to eat my oatmeal and shut up. My father sipped his whiskey with a peaceful expression.

A dog named Flossie looked on in perfect contentment. Uncle Tony, sitting in a ripped vinyl chair that looked as if it had been salvaged from a demolition site, murmured to Flossie a nonstop stream of endearments while he scratched her ears and sucked on his pipe. From time to time, when the conversation threatened to become manageable, Tony would pause from doting on Flossie to shout down a son or daughter, observing that they had never had a single clear thought since being born. A cat walked through, her claws making sounds like tiny high heels on the linoleum, her coat glowing like mink.

Scarcely had I finished my oatmeal when Anthony said I should come with him. I obeyed and out we went through the yard and got in his battered Land Rover. He had offered to take my father as well, but the old man was comfortable in the warm kitchen, and it was a grim morning, chill and wet, out of doors.

I had no idea where we were going, and mostly I didn't care. Anthony was about my age. His chest stood out with muscle from years of farm work. He was a strange mixture of calm and storm. In fact, all of them were. It was an odd fact that though they lived in the middle of nowhere, with utter silence around them as thick as mittens, they all seemed to be somehow overstimulated. The scene in the kitchen had been pandemonium. It had felt like some kind of riot. I was relieved to be in the car, with only Anthony's occasional comments interrupting the drum of the rain. We went through a little town and pulled up by a church.

We got out and Anthony led me around back to a graveyard. The rain was falling at a good rate, but he seemed not to notice. He had on some kind of threadbare field jacket. I followed him until he stopped at a substantial forbidding Victorian tombstone that looked like the door to rot and doom. It was engraved with my name: SHANLEY. I felt the letters like a verdict I would not survive. This was my grandparents' resting place.

He invited me to kneel down in the rain and pray, and did so himself. On my own, this would not have been my first instinct. We knelt side by side, on black gravel, praying before a black stone that looked strangely like the slab in *2001: A Space Odyssey*. I don't know what I prayed for or to. It may have been for an umbrella. I had never met my grandparents, so I had no image or emotional connection to draw on. But kneeling there in the rain, I felt a bond with something dreadful and grand, and I had this thought: *These are my people.*

Over the course of days, I asked for stories about my grandparents. You would think that when dealing with people who talked this much, getting information would be easy, but no. When the subject of my grandparents came up, a sudden circumspection would overcome the source. Tony would look vague. My father would become reticent. My cousins would claim to know nothing. Even my Aunt Mary, who talked like Proust wrote (that is, endlessly), even Mary had little to say.

There was a reason. It seems my grandparents had been, at the very least, scary. My grandfather had gotten along with no one in his family except my father. Even the animals would run away from him. When he wanted the horse, he would have to hide in the house while one of his sons fetched the animal, because if the horse saw my grandfather, the horse would be gone. My grandmother was obese and quarrelsome.

My grandfather constructed barns and furniture, and then my grandmother would gleefully criticize his work until he exploded. They fought constantly, throwing stools, buckets, and whatever else was free. When my grandmother was presented her first grandchild, my sister Kathleen, she tore the pretty bonnet the baby wore off her tiny head, declaring, "It's too good for her!" When she died, they had to take the banister off the staircase from her bedroom. Such was her girth.

It took many conversations for me to gather this unfortunate news about my predecessors. My living family were solid people and thought it wrong to speak ill of the dead. This was the reason their talk became evasive and cloudy when the subject was raised. It was only over the course of many days that a portrait of the couple emerged. They had been poor, illiterate and vindictive. I wondered how such wonderful eccentric folk as I saw around me were able to spring from such impoverished ground. I never got an answer to that.

Life holds its miracles, good erupting from darkness chief among them.

—John Patrick Shanley

This essay was originally published as "The Darkness of an Irish Morning" in the *New York Times* on March 8, 2013.

Outside
Mullingar

———

Production History

Outside Mullingar was originally commissioned and produced by Manhattan Theatre Club (Lynne Meadow, Artistic Director; Barry Grove, Executive Producer), with funds provided by U.S. Trust, in New York City, opening on January 23, 2014. It was directed by Doug Hughes; the set design was by John Lee Beatty, the costume design was by Catherine Zuber, the lighting design was by Mark McCullough, the original music and sound design were by Fitz Patton; the dialect coach was Stephen Gabis, the production stage manager was Winnie Y. Lok, the stage manager was Carlos Maisonet. The cast was:

TONY	Peter Maloney
ANTHONY	Brían F. O'Byrne
AOIFE	Dearbhla Molloy
ROSEMARY	Debra Messing

CHARACTERS

TONY REILLY, seventy-five or so
ANTHONY REILLY, his son, forty-two
AOIFE MULDOON, their neighbor, seventy
ROSEMARY MULDOON, her daughter, thirty-six

TIME/SETTING

Killucan, Ireland, 2008, 2009, 2013.

Scene 1

It's December 2008. The sound of cattle, doves and wind. The bachelor farm kitchen of a cattle and sheep farm outside Kil-lucan, in Ireland. Over the sink, on a shelf, is an old TV. A turf stove sits on a torn linoleum floor. A small table by a window still has some uncleared dishes. A vinyl chair, with stuffing visible here and there, is set up in a nook created by a staircase. The first of two doors opens and shuts, off. The second now opens into the kitchen, revealing Tony Reilly, a wily old Irishman in a serviceable dark suit and Greek fishing cap, followed by Anthony Reilly, his son. Tony is seventy-five or so, and his eyes are sly. Anthony is forty-two, and his eyes are those of an intense dreamer.

ANTHONY: Jesus, what an experience. My heart feels like a stone. It's a physical sensation.

TONY: Why did you do it? That's what I want to know.

5

ANTHONY: The whole half of me cut across the shoulders down is horrible. It's grief, that's what it is.

TONY: We'd be done with it now if it wasn't for you.

ANTHONY: Done with what?

TONY: What do you think? Our obligations. Our social obligations.

ANTHONY: Obligations? There are no obligations.

TONY: All that was left to do was good night, and sorry for your trouble. But you had to say, "Come by."

ANTHONY: Are you that selfish, Daddy?

TONY: I can't be bothered.

ANTHONY: You don't mean it.

TONY: Ah, you're half woman. You'd better see to those dishes now.

ANTHONY: Jesus, you're right. Mother of God, look at this. They'll think us tramps.

TONY: Your mother would die again if she saw the state of this house.

(Anthony puts on an apron and starts washing dishes.)

ANTHONY: Don't mention death. And us staring at poor Christopher Muldoon's headstone this very day.

TONY: It took me back to the last time he died.

ANTHONY: The last time he what?

TONY: Chris Muldoon. The last time he died.

ANTHONY: If this is your notion of humor, no one's laughing.

TONY: Where's me pipe?

ANTHONY: Upstairs. And you're not getting it.

TONY: I'll have it when I want. Muldoon died before.

ANTHONY: Would you stop?

TONY: He was a great one for the pub years ago. Never missed a Sunday with his mates. Until that night his son was born.

ANTHONY: The Muldoons never had a son.

TONY: They did. Years gone by. They had a son, but the poor gossoon was born broken and died a few weeks in.

ANTHONY: I couldn't not know.

6

TONY: It wasn't spoken of.

ANTHONY: Everything's spoken of in Killucan.

TONY: They didn't put it about as the baby was born half size and got smaller from there.

ANTHONY: He shrank?

TONY: Like a sock in the wash. They named him Christopher after his father, and he died right before he was baptized.

ANTHONY: No.

TONY: Yes. Off to limbo he went.

ANTHONY: Don't talk about this when they come.

TONY: So they put it in the paper that Christopher Muldoon was dead, and didn't the lads down in the pub think their mate had passed. They showed up at the wake half pissed, and what do they find sitting there but a little white coffin one foot long. And the one of them cries out, "Jesus! Look at that! Is that all that's left of Chris Muldoon?"

(Tony has a good laugh.)

ANTHONY: They thought it was Chris Muldoon?

TONY: Well, it was and it wasn't.

ANTHONY: Chris Muldoon had a son.

TONY: He did. For a minute. Yer man went a bit daft after that. Took up the shotgun and went to war with the birds.

ANTHONY: He did like to shoot the crows.

TONY: We're lucky there's any left in Ireland. He tore holes in the sky with that gun.

(Anthony is washing dishes. Tony chuckles. Aoife walks in, dressed in black. She's seventy, in bad health, short of breath, walking with a cane, a bit ravaged with grief.)

AOIFE: What's funny?

(Anthony tears off the apron.)

ANTHONY: Are you alright, Aoife?

AOIFE: Alright, is it? Look at me. I'm in pieces. Get the door.

TONY: Aoife, come and sit with me.

AOIFE: Were you having a laugh?

TONY: We were.

ANTHONY: We were not.

AOIFE: What about?

ANTHONY: Can I get you some tea?

AOIFE: I've eaten.

ANTHONY: A stout then?

AOIFE: In the bottle or the can?

ANTHONY: The bottle.

AOIFE: No, thank you. The bottle tastes of glass.

ANTHONY: Does glass have a taste then?

AOIFE: Glass tastes like teeth.

TONY: Oh the taste of glass, sure I know it. It tastes like mirrors.

AOIFE: I've come to think it's not me tasting the glass, but the glass that's tasting me. I see jaws and teeth and meself chewed up like poor Chrissy.

ANTHONY: So no to the stout. Well, I'm making a cup of tea and you'll have one.

TONY: It's an awful thing to get old.

AOIFE: I know. It happened to me.

ANTHONY: You? You're a girl.

AOIFE: I was this morning, but now I'm old.

TONY: When the husband goes, the wife follows, it's true. You'll be dead in a year.

ANTHONY: She will not. She looks perfect.

TONY: Oh, the fruit still looks good when the worm starts his work.

ANTHONY: Shut up.

AOIFE: I'm gasping like an old hurdy-gurdy with the emphysema. I've got the pacemaker on board. You can feel it with your hand. It sticks half out of my chest right where I used to keep the smokes. Justice isn't pretty, is it? Feel it. Put your hand there.

ANTHONY: I will not.

AOIFE: Tony's right. I'll be dead in a year.

TONY: Half a year.

ANTHONY: She will not.

AOIFE: I don't mind. Except to desert Rosemary and leave her orphaned altogether.

ANTHONY: What about you? When are you packing up?

TONY: Me? I'll be dead in two months.

ANTHONY: Just don't. Where is Rosemary?

AOIFE: She's here.

ANTHONY: Where?

AOIFE: Outside.

ANTHONY: In the rain?

AOIFE: She won't smoke in front of me, and she's always smoking, so I never see her. Now let me ask you, Tony, have you signed the farm over to Anthony?

ANTHONY: What? Just like that you ask him?

AOIFE: I'm thinking of my own situation now. What would be best for Rosemary.

ANTHONY: Right.

AOIFE: Or are you going to wait and leave it to him?

ANTHONY: Who else would he leave it to? The others have all fled.

TONY: I haven't made up me mind.

ANTHONY: About what?

TONY: I would have thought yer man Chris Muldoon would have laid out a plan before he was done.

AOIFE: He did. What was his to leave, he left to me.

ANTHONY: As he should have done.

AOIFE: It's only arrangements for Rosemary I'm thinking of now. The future.

ANTHONY: Rosemary's standing out there in the rain?

AOIFE: She is. Smoking. She always manages to find a dry spot though, not so much for herself, as for the smokes.

ANTHONY: Well, she'll catch pneumonia.

AOIFE: No, she's crazy. The cracked ones never get sick. Her father's curse is hers. Stubborn to the point of madness.

ANTHONY: I never noticed it.

AOIFE: That's because you never notice anything, Anthony. You're famous all over Westmeath for what goes by you.

ANTHONY: What do you mean, you don't know if the farm is coming to me? Are you serious?

TONY: I don't see a clear path.

ANTHONY: From where to where?

TONY: From me to you. The way your eyes are set in your face, and the color of them—it has to be said, it's not right.

ANTHONY: Here we go. Are you saying that my eyes are a mistake?

TONY: I'm saying that you come up from some other people. It's as plain as Tuesday. Your eyes are from Limerick.

ANTHONY: My eyes are from Limerick, are they? That I have to listen to this.

TONY: The Reillys are from Cavan.

AOIFE: The Muldoons are from Fermanagh.

TONY: And it's the Kellys that are from Limerick. There's no argument to be made. It's like wool and white paper. You're more Kelly than Reilly.

AOIFE: He has his mother's face, that's true.

ANTHONY: But my name is Reilly. I'm a Reilly.

TONY: No. The Reillys have more bone. You're Kelly. You take after John Kelly, and that man was half ghost and mad as the full moon.

ANTHONY: Stop there.

TONY: I won't stop. You're the same. It's not in you to stand on your ground, Anthony. It has to be said. You never stood up on the farm like a king.

ANTHONY: I've been breaking my back for this place since I was five.

TONY: Not the same.

ANTHONY: As what?

TONY: You don't stand on the land and draw strength from it. As I did. Till Mammy died.

AOIFE: Don't feel bad. Chris Muldoon didn't like farming either. He told me more than once. He only loved life when he was in bed or eating beef. The farm took it out of him.

ANTHONY: The two of you. You know your whole generation has killed this country with your negativity.

TONY: It wasn't us that went boom and bust.

ANTHONY: No, you just went bust and stayed bust.

TONY: Point me towards Heaven then.

ANTHONY: Careful what you say. Heaven might hear.

TONY: I do say it.

ANTHONY: Well, don't!

TONY: Why? Are you going to get weepy?

ANTHONY: You're the one for that!

TONY *(To Aoife)*: He cries at the TV.

ANTHONY: No more. You broke it.

TONY: And good riddance! He made me watch the Olympics till I almost went blind.

ANTHONY: Would you complain about the Olympics now? Nothing suits ya. The Olympics were grand. Weren't they, Aoife?

AOIFE: Chris loved the torch. You know, when they light the torch. He said it was better than Easter Sunday. I didn't care for it.

TONY: And there was no soccer.

ANTHONY: There was. They called it football.

TONY: Not an Irishman on the field.

ANTHONY: Ireland took three medals.

TONY: Not in soccer.

ANTHONY: Nevertheless three medals is not nothing.

TONY: No gold. Two of them bronze. And all in boxing. Sure, we're good with our fists. No surprise there.

ANTHONY: There's more than one way to land a blow.

AOIFE: And the whole show in China, with them parading: "Oh, look at us. We're Chinese." Rosemary was taken with them. Sent away for travel books. But she'll never go. She'll never get further than Mullingar, that one.

ANTHONY: That's it. If only for want of better company, I'm getting Rosemary.

AOIFE: She doesn't like you, you know.

ANTHONY: What?

AOIFE: Rosemary has a grudge with you.

ANTHONY: She does not.

AOIFE: She does.

ANTHONY: She does not.

AOIFE: You pushed her and she fell down.

ANTHONY: What are you talking about? Pushed her? When?
I never did.

AOIFE: You did.

ANTHONY: When?

AOIFE: When she was six. It was your birthday. She was doing
a little ballet and you pushed her down. And she holds it
against you.

ANTHONY: Is that what she says?

AOIFE: She does.

TONY: You pushed a little girl?

ANTHONY: I don't remember, but if I did, I would have been
twelve.

AOIFE: Thirteen. That day.

ANTHONY: Thirteen then.

AOIFE: I wouldn't bring it up. She's still hot about it.

ANTHONY: Why would I bring up something that happened
thirty years ago?

TONY: So you admit it.

ANTHONY: Does it ever seem to you that this country is just too
small?

TONY: Maybe you should emigrate?

ANTHONY: And what would you do with the land if I did?

TONY: Give it to the church.

AOIFE: Well, don't do that.

TONY: If no one loves the land, then why not?

ANTHONY: I love it.

TONY: You don't. I've seen you with your magazines. He's mad
for the machines. He'd sell the land and buy a helicopter
if no one was watching.

ANTHONY: I'd love to get a helicopter. I'd ride it to the moon.

TONY: There. You see. You're not a farming man.

ANTHONY: I'm more the farmer than you ever were.

TONY: You take no joy in it.

ANTHONY: But I do it. Who modernized the shed? You? I don't think so. Who moved the bales from the box shape to the round?

TONY: I don't like the new bales.

ANTHONY: Why not?

TONY: They're too big. You can't sit on them.

ANTHONY: Sit on your chair and thank your Maker for a modern son. You'd be bankrupt and the farm gone if it wasn't for my agricultural mind.

TONY: But you don't love it. There's no joy.

ANTHONY: Don't criticize me, Daddy. Some of us don't have joy. But we do what we must. Is a man who does what he must though he feels no pleasure less of a man than one who's happy? You'd grudge me my magazines, you old cutthroat? Living as I do here with nothing but the rain and cold, and Mammy gone? So I look at the electronics to take my thoughts away. You know I'll tell ya. Sometimes lately I can't breathe in this house. You'd hold back the farm, would ya? You stun me. You stun me.

(Anthony goes out.)

TONY: Well, look at him.

AOIFE: Don't tease him then.

TONY: I wasn't teasing.

AOIFE: You were, and don't. He's sad. You know he feels more deeply than most. God love him. He never got over Fiona.

TONY: He was sixteen.

AOIFE: A tender age.

TONY: He is now forty-two.

AOIFE: Time means nothing. Love is love.

TONY: She never had use for him. I never saw it. The whole thing happened in his mind.

AOIFE: And where else do things happen? We all can't have the love I had. Or you. Look at this. More tears. Oh, where do they come from? What's it all for, Tony?

TONY: Ask a priest.

AOIFE: I've buried husband, son. Was I only born to bury and be buried?

TONY: That's about it maybe.

AOIFE: Don't say it. That leaves off the best bit.

TONY: And what would that be?

AOIFE: The middle. The middle is the best part. The middle of anything is the heart of the thing. I think of Rosemary.

TONY: She's only watching the clock spin, waiting for you to go.

AOIFE: I know.

TONY: But she's waited too long. They both did. Mine and yours.

AOIFE: It's natural.

TONY: But with Rosemary, it's a shame.

AOIFE: She's had no lack of men come by.

TONY: Oh I know. But youth and beauty pass smartly by, and that parade has gone.

AOIFE: You'd think a girl of twenty-five is past prime.

TONY: Twenty-five? She'll never see thirty-five again.

AOIFE: You'll not see tomorrow if you keep talking.

TONY: I will see it. I have a cool eye on tomorrow. The future of this place is what keeps me sharp. And the funeral today reminded me that time is in short supply. Biscuit?

AOIFE: I'm stuffed. But you're not serious what you were saying? You can't begrudge Anthony the farm?

TONY: There's no marriage in the man. He's strange. Stranger than you know. He takes after John Kelly and that's a fact. I'm sworn by an oath or I'd tell ya. So what happens then? When he's gone, it's all gone.

AOIFE: Either way, it's all gone.

TONY: No. There's another route.

AOIFE: What?

TONY: America.

AOIFE: What?

TONY: I have my brother there, Frank, and he has a son. Adam.

AOIFE: You would not.

TONY: I'll do what's right. Watch me. I will.

AOIFE: You can't do it. What would become of Anthony?

TONY: There'd be money for him. He'd move to Dublin and love it.

AOIFE: He'd move to Dublin and die you mean. Who the hell is Adam?

TONY: He's a Reilly. Frank brought him last Christmas. You met him.

AOIFE: The square little fella?

TONY: He loves the land.

AOIFE: I remember him. He looked like a stump.

TONY: He looks like a farmer. He's a Reilly through and through. He has hands like feet.

AOIFE: He laughed at the wrong things.

TONY: He was born to come home, that one.

AOIFE: This is a folly, Tony Reilly, and don't you do it.

TONY: So Rosemary's getting your farm there?

AOIFE: Of course. Who else?

TONY: It makes sense. There's some kind of hope there. She may yet marry a man who has a child. Or if she jumps on it, she could even squeeze one out.

AOIFE: I don't see it.

TONY: Once you're gone, she'll give a fella a chance.

AOIFE: She hates them all.

TONY: She has a better shot than Anthony.

AOIFE: Tony, don't lose faith in your boy.

TONY: I've been patience itself. I gave him his mother's ring three years gone and he's done nothing with it. And he never will. That's not my fault. He has strange ideas.

AOIFE: You're going the wrong way.

TONY: This is my family's farm a hundred and twenty years and it won't stop with Anthony. No, it will not.

AOIFE: Things end when God says they do. *(Stricken)* Oh, I can't believe my Chrissy's gone.

TONY: Aoife.

AOIFE: Half my house is gone.

TONY: Should we speak of it?

AOIFE: What?

TONY: A topic of concern. The topic.

AOIFE: What are you talking about?

TONY: There was no point while Chris was living.

AOIFE: Are you taking a step towards me?

TONY: What? Jesus, no. The land. I'm talking about the land. The strip of forty meters like a blockade in the middle of my driveway, keeping my house from the road.

AOIFE: You have only to open the gate.

TONY: And close it. And open the second gate, and close that as well.

AOIFE: Are you that lazy?

TONY: Have you gotten out of my car in the rain and drowned yourself working those damned gates? And all over a patch of nothing.

AOIFE: It rains on us all.

TONY: I'll give you a fair price for it.

AOIFE: Did you broach this with Chrissy?

TONY: I did, and never had he a word in reply. But he's passed over now.

AOIFE: Just.

TONY: He was a good man, but stubborn.

AOIFE: He was a bulldog. That man would fight the sky.

TONY: He did, and the sky won.

AOIFE: In truth it did. He's gone to God.

TONY: It's mine.

AOIFE: It is not.

TONY: It should be. Can you deny it?

AOIFE: I do deny it.

TONY: The one reason you own that bit a land is hate and spite.

AOIFE: That's two reasons.

TONY: Hate and spite and a love of the upper hand.

AOIFE: What kind of twist is that on the truth? You were down on your luck and Chris took pity.

TONY: There was no pity in it. All I needed was the loan of two hundred pounds and for that he took my right of way.

AOIFE: You sold it to him.

TONY: It was a loan.

AOIFE: It was not. I have a bill of sale.

TONY: I was back to him in six months with the money.

AOIFE: He didn't need the money.

TONY: He didn't need that bit a land, but he held on to it thirty years.

AOIFE: Yes he did.

TONY: Why did he? Why?

AOIFE: Maybe there was no why.

TONY: No. Something went unsaid.

AOIFE: The situation does you no real harm.

TONY: It does you no good.

AOIFE: Leave it. Why go into it now?

TONY: Because my time is almost done.

AOIFE: Tut tut.

TONY: And I need to pass the farm down as it was given me.

AOIFE: To an American?

TONY: He has an Irish passport.

AOIFE: He's no Irishman.

TONY: He means to marry Irish. Some day.

AOIFE: Who'd have him?

TONY: Half the women of Killucan and beyond Killucan.

AOIFE: I'm glad you can speak for so many.

TONY: I need that roadfront back, Aoife.

AOIFE: Why?

TONY: Frank's son Adam won't buy the farm without it.

AOIFE: So he's buying it. Adam is.

TONY: I have to give Anthony a stake. I can't put him out on the road with nothing. I'll get a fair price with Adam and keep the family's name going to boot. But I need access to the road.

AOIFE: I see. Well. I don't own it.

TONY: What?

AOIFE: The frontage Chrissy bought from you I do not own. All the rest is mine, but not that.

TONY: Did he sell it to someone else?

AOIFE: No. He gave it to Rosemary.

TONY: Just the little bit in front of my house? Blocking my house from the road. Just that?

AOIFE: Yes. He signed it over to her when she was a wee girl.

TONY: A girl?

AOIFE: Not more than seven.

TONY: He gave a seven-year-old girl my right of way?

AOIFE: She asked him for it.

TONY: What did she want with it?

AOIFE: It's the spot where Anthony pushed her down. She was all in a rage, and nothing would soothe her but to know he was banished from that spot.

TONY: You mean I've been opening and closing two gates for thirty years to please the pride of a vengeful child?

AOIFE: Yes. And now, if you want that land, you'll have to get around her.

TONY: Talk to her, Aoife. She'll listen to you.

AOIFE: I'm not stepping into this. If she'd been in the Olympics boxing, sure Ireland would have taken the gold.

Scene 2

Outside. The manger. Straw and stone. It's raining, but there's an overhang that shelters. Anthony arrives to find Rosemary smoking her pipe. It's dark.

ANTHONY: Rosemary? What are you doing out here, away from the house?

ROSEMARY: Smoking.

ANTHONY: Out here in the rain?

ROSEMARY: There's a bit of roof.

ANTHONY: And it's dark as tar.

ROSEMARY: I can see.

ANTHONY: You have the eyes of a goat. You're smoking a pipe now?

ROSEMARY: I ran out of cigs. It's Da's ole chimney.

(Anthony goes into the shed and switches on a light.)

ANTHONY: I suppose I can't blame you whatever you choose to do on the night your father died.

ROSEMARY: He died three days ago.

ANTHONY: During the general time that your father died.

ROSEMARY: So I have special rights tonight?

ANTHONY: I suppose.

ROSEMARY: Then I'll use them. Will you answer me a question?

ANTHONY: What?

ROSEMARY: Have you ever heard from Fiona?

ANTHONY: Is the human race against me this night?

ROSEMARY: Don't answer then.

ANTHONY: Never. I have never heard from Fiona since our childhood days.

ROSEMARY: And your heart's still broken?

ANTHONY: Yes.

ROSEMARY: Do you know where she is?

ANTHONY: I do. In Wicklow. With a husband and three daughters.

ROSEMARY: Why didn't you just get over her like other people do?

ANTHONY: I don't know what other people do and I don't care. Why do you do what you do? Why do you stay over there in that lonely house?

ROSEMARY: It's not lonely.

ANTHONY: You should fly. Once your mam . . . Once you're alone. You should make plans to fly away.

ROSEMARY: Why don't you fly?

ANTHONY: It may come to that.

ROSEMARY: Ha. You'll never leave.

ANTHONY: I might. Tony's up to mischief.

ROSEMARY: What kind?

ANTHONY: He says I don't love the farm.

ROSEMARY: Do you?

ANTHONY: He says I'm not a Reilly.

ROSEMARY: Then what are you?

ANTHONY: He claims I'm a Reilly in name, but a Kelly in the face. He's making noises like he might not sign it over.

ROSEMARY: Well, that's not right.

ANTHONY: He's always been half craft. Not like your da, may he rest in peace. He was full on.

ROSEMARY: Till he wasn't. It was me that found him. I looked in on him, and then I was going to go, but for his hand. His one hand lay outside the sheet and I found myself looking at it. And it came across me that there was no life in it and he was dead. Then I called, and Mam came, and her face went white, so I gave her a drink of water. But didn't the glass have his teeth in it.

ANTHONY: No.

ROSEMARY: Oh it was awful. She was wild. She won't drink from a glass since.

ANTHONY: I can testify to that. She said it tastes like teeth.

ROSEMARY: Says it tastes like teeth.

(They laugh.)

ANTHONY: But really. Your da. He was here and now he's not. Where do we go? Do we go into the sky?

ROSEMARY: The ground.

ANTHONY: Then what's the sky for?

ROSEMARY: Now. It's for now.

ANTHONY: Now. Seize the day, is that it? Seize it and do what though? What do you do?

ROSEMARY: Me? I smoke.

ANTHONY: You should quit that.

ROSEMARY: Why?

ANTHONY: I don't know but do it.

ROSEMARY: Girl needs a reason.

(He looks into the night.)

ANTHONY: I hear a voice sometimes when I'm in the fields, and the voice says, "Go."

ROSEMARY: I came upon a patch of white heather this morning.

ANTHONY: White? You did not. That's only in shops.

ROSEMARY: Wild.

ANTHONY: Wild white heather? That's good luck.

ROSEMARY: They say. So is Tony right? Do you not love the farm?

ANTHONY: Love? I hate it for a prison. I came up out of it like a tree and here I am with it around me.

ROSEMARY: Then let Tony do what he wants and follow the voice.

ANTHONY: Do you mean it?

ROSEMARY: I'm saying it.

ANTHONY: Run off. Where? The airport?

ROSEMARY: Take Lufthansa. I hear it's good.

ANTHONY: No. It's all here. It's sitting on top of me.

ROSEMARY: The voice said Go.

ANTHONY: And what am I? St. Joan following voices? My life is fixed down with a rock on each corner.

ROSEMARY: By what?

ANTHONY: There's the green fields, and the animals living off them. And over that there's us, living off the animals. And over that there's that which tends to us and lives off us. Whatever that is, it holds me here. No. The voice I hear in the fields wants me in the fields.

ROSEMARY: Then why does it say go?

ANTHONY: I don't know. Everything doesn't tally.

ROSEMARY: I don't feel the land like you do.

ANTHONY: Count your blessings.

ROSEMARY: Your eyes have pagan things in them sometimes.

ANTHONY: My eyes, is it? Your mother says you're mad.

ROSEMARY: I'm not.

ANTHONY: I am. Should we go in?

ROSEMARY: How are you mad?

ANTHONY: People don't appeal to me that much.

ROSEMARY: That's normal. Who likes people? Nobody.

ANTHONY: I don't know what I'm saying. I'm just more with nature . . . than people. Stories I heard when I was a boy got hold of me. Should we go in then?

ROSEMARY: I'm grieving.

ANTHONY: Of course you are. When my mother died, Jesus, I couldn't see colors anymore.

ROSEMARY: My mam's falling apart. She needs new hips, but she can't get 'em 'cause her lungs and heart are cooked. She's not long for it.

ANTHONY: You think not?

ROSEMARY: I know.

ANTHONY: And will you take over the farm?

ROSEMARY: I will.

ANTHONY: But you can't.

ROSEMARY: I must though.

ANTHONY: It's too much.

ROSEMARY: You do it.

ANTHONY: I don't. And what I do get done, it murders me. It's no work for a woman, I'll tell you that.

ROSEMARY: I can hold my own.

ANTHONY: What about pulling calves?

ROSEMARY: I'll hire someone then.

ANTHONY: Takes money.

ROSEMARY: We're alright. What would Tony do with the farm if he didn't leave it to you?

ANTHONY: He might give it to the church.

ROSEMARY: He's too cheap. He'd sell.

ANTHONY: He wouldn't get his price for it.

ROSEMARY: Why not?

ANTHONY: Who would take it on without the road?

ROSEMARY: Ah. Right.

ANTHONY: No one would sign on without that strip of land by the road.

ROSEMARY: Maybe not.

ANTHONY: Be realistic. No one else would open two gates just to get to your own front door.

ROSEMARY: You do.

ANTHONY: And look at me.

ROSEMARY: So you're lucky then.

ANTHONY: How am I lucky?

ROSEMARY: He can't sell without the right of way. He's too cheap to give it to the church. So you'll come to it by default.

ANTHONY: Unless your mammy sells it back to him now that your da's gone.

ROSEMARY: Why would she do that?

ANTHONY: Well, it's the right thing.

ROSEMARY: I don't know.

ANTHONY: Oh you do. It was part of our farm for well wide of a hundred years.

ROSEMARY: And then it wasn't.

ANTHONY: It does your place no good.

ROSEMARY: I think it does.

ANTHONY: You couldn't graze one heifer on that patch. Half of it's taken up with fence.

ROSEMARY: Do you mind it so much?

ANTHONY: I do. At the first gate I see my father's stupidity, and at the second, your man's greed. May he rest in peace.

ROSEMARY: Greed is it? That little bit cost us two hundred pounds.

ANTHONY: Even thirty years ago two hundred pounds was nothing.

ROSEMARY: It was two hundred pounds. He could've bought himself a new shotgun.

ANTHONY: God love him, him with the shotgun. He'd go after the crows like Satan.

ROSEMARY: He loved hating the crows.

ANTHONY: He did.

ROSEMARY: He was perfect.

ANTHONY: He was, he was. Do you hate me?

ROSEMARY: Why do you ask?

ANTHONY: I hear you hate me. Your mam said.

ROSEMARY: Well, she's talking a lot tonight, isn't she? I don't hate you. I just don't like you.

ANTHONY: Why not?

ROSEMARY: I'm fed up. You're a bit of a lump.

ANTHONY: How's that?

ROSEMARY: You never do anything.

ANTHONY: I work all day and half the night.

ROSEMARY: To keep things going on the way they already were. But where's your stamp?

ANTHONY: I'm not in the business of stamping. I'm in the business of carrying on what was going on when I stepped on the bus.

ROSEMARY: But then it's like you're nobody.

ANTHONY: I don't need to shout my name. God knows me. I'd as soon go unnoticed.

ROSEMARY: But you have to push back, man, now and then, or they'll eat you alive, the people of this world. You can't let people, Tony or no one, destroy your chance. Go in there and face him down.

ANTHONY: I don't like a fight.

ROSEMARY: Who does?

ANTHONY: Half of Ireland. Just not me.

ROSEMARY: See beyond the fight to the prize then.

ANTHONY: It's not in me to live that way.

ROSEMARY: So you'd let him run ruin over you?

ANTHONY: Maybe. I don't know. Oh, get out of this place why don't you? The land isn't holding you.

ROSEMARY: It is though.

ANTHONY: Don't be a lump yourself. You saw the white heather. Let it be a sign. Get past Mullingar. I'm useless but not you. Go somewhere and set up fresh.

ROSEMARY: I'll do what I want and you can go to the devil!

ANTHONY: What are you hot about?

ROSEMARY: Trying to push me out.

ANTHONY: I'm the one on the point of being driven out maybe.

ROSEMARY: Maybe. Have you ever seen *Swan Lake*?

ANTHONY: What's that?

ROSEMARY: A ballet.

ANTHONY: A ballet? I've never seen a ballet.

ROSEMARY: Alright. I'm the White Swan.

ANTHONY: When did you see a ballet?

ROSEMARY: My da took me to one.

ANTHONY: Doesn't sound like him.

ROSEMARY: It was him. He took me to *Swan Lake* and he told me I was the White Swan. And so I am.

ANTHONY: I thought he hated birds.

ROSEMARY: Just crows.

ANTHONY: A man like that at the ballet. I guess I never knew him.

ROSEMARY: To watch him walk was to know there was grace in the world. He had the blood of kings in him.

ANTHONY: He kept his counsel like a king. That's sure. No one knew his mind.

ROSEMARY: I did. He wasn't much of a talker, but he always had his reasons. As do I.

ANTHONY: Then tell me this if you know. Why did he buy that right of way?

ROSEMARY: Because your da came begging.

ANTHONY: You'd like to think so. My man just wanted a loan is all.

ROSEMARY: Either way.

ANTHONY: There was no hat in hand.

ROSEMARY: Bloody hell, his hand was out.

ANTHONY: Would you stand there and lord it over us?

ROSEMARY: Have you never heard of gratitude?

ANTHONY: I'll tell you what I've never heard. I've never heard a decent word from you or yours on the subject of your family's shortcoming!

ROSEMARY: Shortcoming? What shortcoming?

ANTHONY: Sure if you want I can name it! The Muldoon's larceny.

ROSEMARY: The Muldoon's what?

ANTHONY: It should wake you at night. What your people have done!

ROSEMARY: What WE'VE done?! What have we done? You should thank Christ for a good neighbor!

ANTHONY: Bollocks to that! You've had us by the throat for thirty years with your landgrabbing and why? Why did your da want our right of way?

ROSEMARY *(Overlapping)*: For me! For me! You eegit boy! You pushed me down, that's why! You shoved me down and left me crying in the yellow grass. And I would have mine back I would, and ran to my da. So now you have two gates between you and what's yours, and I hope you like it, because there's none to blame but yourself!

ANTHONY: You don't mean it.

ROSEMARY: I do.

ANTHONY: Jesus, Mary, it was you behind that?

ROSEMARY: You shoved me like I was nothing.

ANTHONY: I don't even remember the day.

ROSEMARY: I remember. And I own that parcel and you do not.

ANTHONY: You mean your mam.

ROSEMARY: No. Me. I own it. And I'll never sell it.

ANTHONY: Why not?

ROSEMARY: Because MY voice says no.

ANTHONY: Fine. Do what you want then. The lot of ya are too much for me altogether.

ROSEMARY: Because you won't fight for what's yours. Why don't you move to Wicklow? You could moon after your lost love till death takes you.

ANTHONY: I'll ignore ya now.

ROSEMARY: Nothing new there.

ANTHONY: I don't understand you. Why bring up Fiona?

ROSEMARY: The Black Swan.

ANTHONY: What do you do with your time? Why have you never married?

ROSEMARY: Why haven't you?

ANTHONY: I was ruined after Fiona.

ROSEMARY: Fiona, Fiona.

ANTHONY: I know. But there it is.

ROSEMARY: Well, I'm thinking of going to China.

ANTHONY: Just like that.

ROSEMARY: That's right. In a flash.

ANTHONY: Fine. Have a nice trip. Take Lufthansa. When?

ROSEMARY: When I'm ready.

ANTHONY: The Olympics caught your fancy, hey?

ROSEMARY: I like the Chinese. They're proud.

ANTHONY: Why do you look at me when you say that?

ROSEMARY: Because your pride is where?

ANTHONY: What would I be proud about?

ROSEMARY: You're right. What would ya? I'm stumped.

ANTHONY: I'm just a long suffering man. It's no one's fault. I'm not to be understood, not even by me.

ROSEMARY: Oh, what are you now? Deep waters?

ANTHONY: I'm nothing. You saw your father gone as I have this day. Chris Muldoon gone! He was part of everything. Now that part's where? Like the fog wiped from a glass. And what am I, given that? A tiny thing certainly. Jesus. My own father scheming to rob me of my farm.

ROSEMARY: Then fight for it.

ANTHONY: Or wash my hands.

ROSEMARY: So you're Pontius Pilate?

ANTHONY: Maybe so. It's too much. There's no reward for the work I've done and it must be that I don't deserve any. It must be that I've done nothing right.

ROSEMARY: You mean you've done nothing.

ANTHONY: I'm mad tired for a man who's done nothing.

ROSEMARY: Then wake up and live. Oh, do what you want. You always have. And you see where it's gotten you. You're on the point of being pushed out.

ANTHONY: Pushed out? When was I in? Among people? They'd eat the legs out from under ya. You know. You know what? I tell ya. I've had enough. I'm going flying.

ROSEMARY: Flying is it? Where's your wings?

ANTHONY: Walking, I mean.

ROSEMARY: Go then. Stay off the road.

ANTHONY: No road for me. Off into the fields. I'll see you at church. Or I won't. Turn off the lights when you're done.

ROSEMARY: Take note of your cattle. You're like a brother to them.

(Anthony is gone.)

ANTHONY *(Off)*: I'll see you at church.
ROSEMARY: "There's the green fields, and the animals living off them. And over that there's us, living off the animals. And over us there's that which tends to us." When you say those things, Anthony, I know that I have a soul.

(She heads back toward the house.)

Good luck to him. And to me.

Scene 3

Back in the kitchen we find Tony and Aoife.

TONY: It was a fine turnout. It was, though.

AOIFE: It's a shame, the lack of parking at our church. They should charge.

TONY: They should charge, should they? Half of Killucan would renounce the faith.

AOIFE: What grade of faith have they then?

TONY: Not much.

AOIFE: And you? Do you have faith?

TONY: Me? I'm barely devout. It was Mary kept the candles lit.

AOIFE: I believe.

TONY: In what?

AOIFE: I believe in everything.

TONY: You do not.

AOIFE: I believe in everything. There she is. It's time we were off.

TONY: Stay on your chair.

AOIFE: No. This is it. I'm up.

(The outer door opens and shuts. The inner door opens and Rosemary enters.)

ROSEMARY: Back up. Sit down again.

TONY: Is Anthony behind you?

ROSEMARY: He went walking in the fields. Or flying.

TONY: Oh Jesus, once he starts in with that, he won't be seen till morning.

AOIFE: We should say our good-byes, Rosemary.

ROSEMARY: No. Stay down. I'm going to make tea.

(She sets about making tea.)

AOIFE: We should leave Tony sleep.

ROSEMARY: No we shouldn't.

TONY: Alright then. I'd have a cup.

AOIFE: What's that look on you?

ROSEMARY: I hope you have no part in this?

AOIFE: In what?

ROSEMARY: What we say now will never be repeated. Tell me there's no truth in what I just heard.

AOIFE: What did you hear?

ROSEMARY: This is Anthony's farm.

TONY: Oh, Jesus. Don't involve yourself, Rosemary.

AOIFE: Tony's right, Rosemary. This is their own business.

ROSEMARY: Steer clear, Mother. Tony Reilly, do yourself a service and do not cross me.

TONY: Easy. Don't overstep now.

ROSEMARY: Since Mary died, your judgment, which was never good, has faltered worse.

AOIFE: She's right about that, Tony.

TONY: She's nothing. I think I can manage my own farm.

ROSEMARY: If that were true, you would own it. To the road.

TONY: I've heard your name's on that strip of land, Rosemary. And I can tell you now, you will be selling that to me.

AOIFE: I told him it's yours. Don't fault me.

ROSEMARY: I don't. *(To Tony)* I fault you. Why would you think of denying Anthony what's his?

TONY: Leave it.

ROSEMARY: If you want to talk to me about the road, you will talk to me about Anthony.

TONY: What there is to say I won't say. I am bound by an oath, made on a Bible, not to speak of certain things.

ROSEMARY: About Anthony?

TONY: His mother made me swear. Have faith that I know what I'm about.

ROSEMARY: I have no such faith. You've kept him down all his life. And you've done it with the promise of this farm.

TONY: Not a word of truth. I've shielded him on every side. And his interests will be seen to, but the farm will not be his.

ROSEMARY: You have no idea what you're up against, Tony Reilly. You might as well try to stop the calendar from naming the days. I've been older than all of you since I was born, and sure I ache for my own youth. I pray the day may yet come, but not at the price of now.

AOIFE: What are you talking at?

ROSEMARY: When a person knows what will be, and I have always known, the like of you should stand aside.

AOIFE: What are you saying? What do you know?

ROSEMARY: Anthony Reilly and I were born on two farms side by side, and we will die side by side. And no old fool trying to show his muscle at sunset will bungle that.

AOIFE: Rosemary, you have secrets of your own, and once they're out, they're out.

ROSEMARY: I have no secrets. I buried my dear father today, and I'll lose no more.

TONY: Are you in love with Anthony?

ROSEMARY: More than love.

TONY: Don't be.

ROSEMARY: I don't care what happens beyond one thing. I will be on the one farm and he will be on the next.

AOIFE: Rose.

ROSEMARY: Mam, look at me and take pity. You will leave me soon.

AOIFE: Sure it's true. I can't deny it.

ROSEMARY: I feel that grief never more than today. But what preserves me is knowing there are safe roads after.

TONY: He's not normal.

ROSEMARY: I don't care what he is, and if you're bound by an oath, keep it! I don't care about anything but that that man have his land and my house be hard by!

AOIFE: Rosemary.

TONY: He'll never marry.

ROSEMARY: Then neither will I. And he will be in his house and I will be in mine. Here's your tea.

(She serves the tea.)

AOIFE: There is much of your father in you.

ROSEMARY: I'm proud to know it.

AOIFE: Two bulldogs.

ROSEMARY: No, I'm a swan.

TONY: I will not let this farm die with Anthony.

ROSEMARY: "You will not do this." "You will not do that." So what will you do?

AOIFE: He means to sell it to his brother's son.

ROSEMARY: In America?

TONY: He'll come and take over.

ROSEMARY: And go through the two gates?

TONY: He wants the road.

ROSEMARY: I'm here to tell you he will never get it.

TONY: You will not tell me how to dispose of my property!

ROSEMARY: And you'll have no sway over mine! Drink your tea.

TONY: Don't order me in my own house!

ROSEMARY: No one owns a house.

TONY: I own mine.

ROSEMARY: It was handed to you.

TONY: I gave my life to it.

ROSEMARY: And Anthony his.

TONY: He's not a Reilly.

ROSEMARY: Is that what you're about? Your name?

TONY: He takes after his mother's father, John Kelly.

AOIFE: He does. In the face.

TONY: And in the head. John Kelly put his dog on trial for slander.

ROSEMARY: When was that? A hundred years ago?

TONY: Less than seventy.

ROSEMARY: You're the one who's daft.

TONY: Say what you want. Blood will tell.

ROSEMARY: I think it's talking right now a lot of bloody nonsense.

TONY: Anthony doesn't love the farm.

ROSEMARY: What's got hold of you isn't love, old man!

TONY: Who do you think you are?

ROSEMARY: It's pride.

AOIFE: She's right, Tony. You're out of bounds.

TONY: Oh, you're the referee now?

AOIFE: What mother isn't? Now stop trying to bully the room.

TONY: This is my kitchen!

ROSEMARY: And look at it! You're lucky you're not poisoned with the dirt! Do the cattle eat at the table and drink from this sink? There's grease on the wall and a pizza box under the chair! Now drink your tea, you damn savage! You can't be the master of what comes after your time, and your time is nigh well done.

AOIFE: Now don't say a thing like that. It's morbid.

ROSEMARY: If he can play at destiny, so can I. Promise me you'll drop this plan or I swear by the stars, I'll kill you meself.

TONY: I'll promise nothing.

ROSEMARY: Do you think I won't lay hands on you? I'll deal you a mortal blow!

AOIFE: Rosemary!

TONY: If Anthony were a man through and through, if he were a Reilly, he would have at me himself.

ROSEMARY: If you were a man down to your heart, you would not have hurt him with your loveless ways.

TONY: What are you talking about?

ROSEMARY: It's Anthony who loves those fields. Not you. So what if his love makes him suffer? You just want to go on and on. You're selfish.

AOIFE: And what are you?

ROSEMARY: I'm strength. For now.

TONY: He'll never be the man I am.

ROSEMARY: Well, thank God for that. He's done everything for you. You've sat here like a king for twenty years. When was the last time you stayed up with a ewe or clipped the hedge or even killed a rat? You're fooling no one with that captain's hat. Anthony runs the show and you're nothing but the dummy in the window.

TONY: I've earned some rest.

ROSEMARY: Lie down! Who's stopping you?

TONY: But he'll never marry. Look at it. The place would go in auction. It's not right.

AOIFE: Trust in God, Tony. Sure life has its surprises.

ROSEMARY: That it does. I have been to the doctor and I have frozen my eggs!

AOIFE: What?

TONY: You what? Mother of God!

ROSEMARY: So. Surprises, as you say.

AOIFE: Frozen your eggs?

TONY: To the purpose of what?

ROSEMARY: I will keep my options alive.

AOIFE: Jesus, Rosemary, be careful. Don't rampage over the natural order of nature.

ROSEMARY: What nature? It's only my own life I'm playing with.

AOIFE: Your rights then. You can't just rage forward without a road.

ROSEMARY: I know where I'm going.

AOIFE: Well, I hope things go your way. Anthony is a bit slow.

TONY: Slow is it? You should have frozen your whole body if you're waiting for that one.

ROSEMARY: I believe he will come to me.

TONY: He'll never marry.

AOIFE: You don't know that.

TONY: I have reason to think it.

ROSEMARY: The farm goes to Anthony. Say it. Say it.

AOIFE: Don't answer wrong with wrong, Rosemary. Don't bully the man.

(Rosemary takes another tack with Tony.)

ROSEMARY: Think. Of his mother.

TONY: Don't.

ROSEMARY: Think of his mother. Do you remember his mother?

TONY: Remember her? What are you saying? She was my life!

AOIFE: She's right, Tony. That's the question. What would his mother want? What would Mary want?

TONY: She's gone. I can't be thinking that way.

ROSEMARY: Sitting by that stove she'd be. Her ghost is there to see right now.

AOIFE: And Anthony on her knee.

ROSEMARY: By the stove with a piece of turf in her hand. What did she care except for her children?

AOIFE: Sure Anthony was the apple of her eye.

ROSEMARY: And she was a Kelly.

AOIFE: Through and through.

ROSEMARY: And what would Mary Kelly say if she saw this farm taken from her only son BECAUSE he was a Kelly?

TONY: I can't think about it.

AOIFE: What was that song she'd sing while she washed a dish? *(Sings)* "And we'll all go together . . ."

AOIFE AND ROSEMARY *(Singing)*: ". . . to pull wild mountain thyme . . ."

TONY: Stop! Stop! Jesus!

(Aoife and Rosemary break off from singing.)

AOIFE: Sure she was love itself and Anthony was her baby boy.

TONY: I'm only trying to do what's right.

ROSEMARY: Right for who?

TONY: For the farm.

AOIFE: The farm doesn't know a thing about right, and it won't know. You're trying to serve the Reillys, at the expense of the Kellys, even if doing so, Tony, would overturn the living issue of your one true love.

ROSEMARY: Do you know why my da went to war with the crows, Tony? He was shaking his fist. His son failed to live, and he was shaking his fist. You have a son. You want more than that from the sky? Are you after being struck down? Well, are you?

TONY: I hope you never know what it is to be old. And I know you'll never understand what it is to be a man. But alright.

ROSEMARY: Alright what?

TONY: Anthony gets the farm.

AOIFE: Thanks be to God.

ROSEMARY: Good.

TONY: But mark my words. He is John Kelly all over again, and that man talked to turkeys about politics.

AOIFE: Well, it was a long time ago.

ROSEMARY: It was.

AOIFE: Can we go home before the battery in my pacemaker just runs down to nothing?

ROSEMARY: We can. Anthony's out there in the fields somewhere. I like knowing that. We'll go home. Where I'm to wait. Though it be years.

AOIFE: Good enough! May patience and silence rule the world.

(Fade to darkness. Music. An instrumental version of "Wild Mountain Thyme" plays.)

Scene 4

Darkness. We hear Tony.

TONY: Anthony! Anthony!

(The lights come up as Anthony enters in old pajamas. Tony is lying sick in bed. There's an oxygen tube under his nose.)

ANTHONY: I'm coming! I'm coming, Da. Are you alright?
TONY: Bring me my pipe.
ANTHONY: Are you serious? Your pipe? You can't have a pipe.
TONY: I will have it.
ANTHONY: Go back to sleep. You can't smoke with the oxygen.

(Tony takes off the tube.)

TONY: I don't want the oxygen. Get this off me.

ANTHONY: What are you doing? You need that.

TONY: I don't need it. Roll that tank out of my room. I mean it. Do it. I hate the sight of it.

(Anthony complies.)

ANTHONY: Alright. I'll do it. The nurse will have my head though.

TONY: The nurse won't come till morning. With that face of hers.

ANTHONY: She'll smell the smoke.

TONY: Her perfume's worse. We're not living for her. Fill the pipe.

ANTHONY: It's late.

TONY: That it is. I saw a star out the window. Down near the ground. Good. Light it for me.

(Anthony does, and hands it to Tony, who puffs it blissfully and then coughs. And then laughs.)

I'm choking.

ANTHONY: I told ya.

TONY: It doesn't matter. I like the smell, and the pipe in me hand. Sit by me, Son.

(Anthony sits.)

I'm sorry to be leaving you, Anthony.

ANTHONY: Don't say it.

TONY: I'm sorry. It's a lonely spot here at lane's end and it will be hard to face the morning when I'm gone.

(Anthony wipes his eyes.)

ANTHONY: Jesus.

TONY: The farm is yours now, and I'm sorry to be leaving it to you not as it was given me.

ANTHONY: Don't think of it. It's nothing.

TONY: There was reason. When I asked Mam to marry, sure I had nothing to call my own. The ring I gave her was but brass, though she took it like diamonds. Listen, Son. Your mam. I didn't love her.

ANTHONY: What are you saying?

TONY: The truth.

ANTHONY: No.

TONY: I needed a wife, and Mary would have me. But there was no love in it.

ANTHONY: Sure what are you saying? You loved her.

TONY: No. I was without those feelings. The want and loneliness had gotten in me and I looked at people like they were work. I don't know why she said yes. I thought maybe she wanted her own kitchen, as poor as ours was. She made a garden for vegetables so she could see it in the morning, and she'd wait for me by the front door when I came down the old boreen by night. I walked by her half the time without so much as a nod. She bore me children. Trish and Audrey. Then you. And I felt nothing. Till one day something gave way. Out in the fields and the wet grass, the quiet hand of God touched me so soft I thought it was the breeze. Something came to save me, Son, and it will come for you, too. I'd drive out with the feed in the morning and split open the bag into the trough, and the cattle would walk forward . . . I can't name the day. The cattle were there. The rain let up. The sun shone . . . The sun shone on me. And I started in singing. Just like that. That old song. Mam's song. "Wild Mountain Thyme." Do you know it?

ANTHONY: Sure I do.

TONY *(Sings)*: "And we'll all go together . . ."

(Anthony sings with him.)

TONY AND ANTHONY *(Singing)*: ". . . to pull wild mountain thyme . . ."

(They stop.)

TONY: The sun shone on me. And I laughed 'cause I saw *me* singing, and I had never been that man. Never! Singing in the field?! All the days are alike on a farm, and yet of a sudden the drudgery I had known since birth lifted off me and a joy came up into me out of the land. Out of all of it. The cattle and the sky. And when I went home to the house, a moment came there, too, where all of it, you, the girls, her, even the house itself, all of it came to life in me. But it started out there in the fields that had been lonely. When the sun shone on me. And I knew it was her. Mary. Somehow she was my way into the farm and all else besides. So I sold off the bit by the road to Muldoon for two hundred quid, went into town and bought her a real ring of gold, and took the brass one from her. And oh what days we had thereafter. Times in the kitchen. In every room. And I'm going to her now, Son, 'cause I know she's waiting by that old front door for me yet. Can you forgive me, Anthony?

ANTHONY: For what? Selling the right of way? It's nothing.

TONY: Yes. But more. For having no faith that you would find your own way, be your own man. And most of all, for making light of your good heart. *(Takes his hand)* Am I proud of you too late?

ANTHONY: No, no. I don't want you to die.

TONY: I'm sorry I sold the bit by the road and left you with two gates. And that I thought of taking the rest from you. I was no good after Mam died. She was my North Star. Forgive me.

ANTHONY: There's nothing to forgive.

TONY: Forgive me now, Son, for all of it. All my shortcomings. The things I didn't say. However I hurt you. I want to die with the slate clean between us.

ANTHONY: Surely I forgive everything.

(He takes Tony in his arms.)

TONY: I love you, Son. I can't say it enough.

ANTHONY: I love you, my daddy. My daddy. My daddy. Sure I always have.

(The embrace ends.)

TONY: Thank you then. Good man. You better take the pipe.

(Anthony takes the pipe.)

You were a good son.

ANTHONY: Thank you, Da.

TONY: I have faith that love will find you. Out in those fields where you wander. God bless you.

ANTHONY: And you.

TONY: I'll sleep now.

ANTHONY: You want the oxygen?

TONY: I'll try without.

(Anthony turns off the light and goes.)

Scene 5

Out by the shed. A year later. A sunny day. Anthony comes out with a pail of turf to discover Rosemary with a covered dish. She's caught smoking, and flicks the butt.

ROSEMARY: Anthony.
ANTHONY: Rosemary. Still smoking.
ROSEMARY: I brought you some stew.

   (She sits it down.)

ANTHONY: I can cook.
ROSEMARY: You don't though. Now that Mam's gone, I've no one to do for. Keeps me busy.
ANTHONY: Right.
ROSEMARY: The sun's out. Good walking weather.
ANTHONY: One place is the same as another.

ROSEMARY: How can you say it? I was down at the bog cutting turf and the heather is everywhere.

ANTHONY: Cutting your own turf?

ROSEMARY: Who else?

ANTHONY: A bit late.

ROSEMARY: I got to it.

ANTHONY: That's a two-man job.

ROSEMARY: Or one-woman.

ANTHONY: That's the world now.

ROSEMARY: What?

ANTHONY: Men are useless.

ROSEMARY: It's not so.

ANTHONY: What's a man for? What's his place?

ROSEMARY: That's for you to say.

ANTHONY: Is it? I know, you know.

ROSEMARY: About what?

ANTHONY: My da told me.

ROSEMARY: Told you what?

ANTHONY: How you went at him over the farm.

ROSEMARY: Oh that. He was talking blather, may he rest in peace. The farm's yours, as it should be.

ANTHONY: You shouldn't have done that.

ROSEMARY: Why not?

ANTHONY: You spoke for me.

ROSEMARY: You wouldn't speak for yourself.

ANTHONY: I said as much as I wanted.

ROSEMARY: It wasn't enough.

ANTHONY: Well maybe the quiet around a thing is as important as the thing itself.

ROSEMARY: Do you still hear the voice in the fields?

ANTHONY: I don't know.

ROSEMARY: You have the farm.

ANTHONY: I do.

ROSEMARY: Are you happy?

ANTHONY: No.

ROSEMARY: Why not go ahead and be happy?

ANTHONY: I don't know how.

ROSEMARY: There's nothing in the way.

ANTHONY: No?

ROSEMARY: There's no one left to catch you laughing, Anthony.

ANTHONY: That's true.

ROSEMARY: How many days do we have where the sun shines?

ANTHONY: Not too many. Are you alright then?

ROSEMARY: Yes, I am.

ANTHONY: With just you up there in the house?

ROSEMARY: What about you?

ANTHONY: You know, I've been having such dreams! I've been dreaming about everyone who ever lived.

ROSEMARY: That's a lot.

ANTHONY: Ancestors and more than that. The whole wide idea, the history of people. And me at the front of them, like the leader of a marching band. Jesus, I sat up in me bed and I didn't know what to make of it. Here I am, alone as a castaway, and my night is spilling over with people. We're known to each other quite the while now.

ROSEMARY: We are.

ANTHONY: And now we're at the front of the group. Have you thought about what I said?

ROSEMARY: Which? We never speak. It's been a year. I'm over in me house with nothing to do if you want to come by.

ANTHONY: I see you at church.

ROSEMARY: I wouldn't go if you didn't. I hate the Bible. They should call it The Book of Awful Stories.

ANTHONY: Have you no faith?

ROSEMARY: I do have faith, though I don't know how I came by it.

ANTHONY: It's just you now. Nothing holds you here. You should go.

ROSEMARY: Leave this place?

ANTHONY: Why not?

ROSEMARY: Do you want me to?

ANTHONY: I think you should.

ROSEMARY: I'll think about it.

ANTHONY: Do.

ROSEMARY: Come by the house sometime.

ANTHONY: I will maybe.

ROSEMARY: You won't. Girl needs a chat.

ANTHONY: I'd better take this in. I thank you for it.

ROSEMARY: Alright.

ANTHONY: You should quit the smokes.

(He takes the covered dish toward the house. She calls after him.)

ROSEMARY: It's a grand day for a walk.

(He's gone. She stands there, looking after him. She mutters.)

And those days are few.

Scene 6

The lights change. We hear distant thunder and rain. We are in the field outside the Muldoon house, which is lit up. Anthony is wearing a ratty old oilcloth coat and has a metal detector and headset. He approaches, hesitates. Rosemary comes out the door holding a shawl over her head.

ROSEMARY: Anthony! I see ya! You've been seen now!
ANTHONY: Go in!
ROSEMARY: Come in! Don't you dare turn back!
ANTHONY: What are you doing? Don't come out!
ROSEMARY: Come on then. It's too late. I've seen you now. Come in before I drown.

(He follows her in.)

Scene 7

The year is 2013. A steady rain outside. The Muldoon farm's kitchen. It is neat and well kept. Rosemary is ushering in Anthony. He's dripping. She throws off the shawl.

ROSEMARY: Come in then. Give me the coat.

ANTHONY: I'm fine.

ROSEMARY: Give me the coat. Leave your Wellies off.

ANTHONY: I can't stay.

ROSEMARY: Take them off. That's it. One, the other, good. And this is the summer weather! Jesus, look at the rain. Is Noah behind you? That's it. You're in. Oh, Mother of Mercy, don't look, Anthony, for the love of God! The house is in ruins! You'll think me a clotty woman, that's certain.

ANTHONY: Not a bit. It's not a bad time?

ROSEMARY: What would I be about? Other than cleaning, which I haven't done in weeks.

ANTHONY: What are you saying? You're daft. The floor is gleaming. It's sterilized.

ROSEMARY: It is not. You're blind. And the walls are yellow with old smoke. Me mother left me with this coughing stove and the linoleum like sludge.

ANTHONY: Your mother will never be dead while you're alive, Rosemary. You see disaster where others see green fields.

ROSEMARY: I can't deny it. If it weren't for rare signs from Heaven, I'd have nothing in me mind but doom.

ANTHONY: Rare signs from Heaven?

ROSEMARY: Few they are. Sit down before your legs go. Here's a towel for your head.

ANTHONY: That's alright, I have a handkerchief.

(He pulls out an awful handkerchief.)

ROSEMARY: How long has that been in your pocket?

ANTHONY: I don't know.

ROSEMARY: It's half alive. Take the towel and give that over.

(She takes it with a pair of tongs.)

I'll wash it if it doesn't run off.

ANTHONY: Don't bother with me. I can't stay. You know, I'll come back.

ROSEMARY: You'll come back, will you? It's your first time in my house in three years. You hang outside like a wild creature when you come at all.

ANTHONY: Why come in? All houses are strange, are they not?

ROSEMARY: What are you saying?

ANTHONY: It's like being nailed in a crate.

ROSEMARY: My house?

ANTHONY: Any house.

ROSEMARY: You're having me on. Where would you stay, in the rain? Put down that weed whacker and rest your bones.

ANTHONY: It's not a weed whacker. It's the finest metal detector known.

ROSEMARY: People think you're after bombs from Pakistan with that rig.

ANTHONY: Can't a man have a hobby without calling down Judgment Day?

ROSEMARY: Sure, I've seen you roaming the cow paths with that electric thing as often as not. You're becoming famous in the wrong way. What are you after besides the odd treasure?

ANTHONY: Unexpected stuff. Coins maybe.

ROSEMARY: If you want coins, I've got 'em spilling out of the dish there.

ANTHONY: Older coins than that. And odd bits. Metal buttons. Last week I found the keys to a Jaguar.

ROSEMARY: Now you just need the car and you're off to the races. Would you take a Guinness from the bottle?

ANTHONY: It's no use. I'm just here for the minute.

ROSEMARY: You'll visit with me or I'll know why. They say this new bottle Guinness is as good as the pub, but that's a lie. But it isn't too bad maybe.

ANTHONY: Does it taste of glass?

ROSEMARY: It does.

(They share a laugh.)

ANTHONY: Don't open it. I'm going.

ROSEMARY: I'm going to open it.

ANTHONY: Don't.

ROSEMARY: It's done. I've opened it.

ANTHONY: Jesus.

ROSEMARY: It's useless but to drink now.

ANTHONY: Alright, if you will open it, if you must open it, if you've opened it, share it with me.

ROSEMARY: Me? I couldn't.

ANTHONY: Pour it out in two glasses.

ROSEMARY: You're only saying that to divide the time in half you'll stay.

ANTHONY: I'm telling ya. Sit and share it or I won't touch it.

ROSEMARY: Alright then, Anthony. Two glasses. You're a demon tempting me with the drink.

(He puts aside his detector and headset.)

ANTHONY: I'm no worse than the weather.

ROSEMARY: Well, we know how bad that is.

ANTHONY: Sure it's a great day for the rope alright.

ROSEMARY: What do you mean?

ANTHONY: It's a great day to be hanging from the rope.

ROSEMARY: Don't even joke about the rope and the suicide with half the country hanging from the trees and bridges.

ANTHONY: It's me joking, that's all.

ROSEMARY: It's not funny, with the Celtic Tiger belly up and people leaping off castles and cliffs.

ANTHONY: I should jump meself and have done.

ROSEMARY: The Chinese say if you kill yourself, your ghost is trapped to earth till it can tempt another to do the same. Imagine that. Ghosts pushing at us to destroy ourselves.

ANTHONY: The Chinese, is it? You still on that? Have there been many of them bothering you?

ROSEMARY: They believe awful things. I read a book. I'll never go there after all. Do you think about it?

ANTHONY: What?

ROSEMARY: Killing yourself.

ANTHONY: What? No. Why? Do you think about it?

ROSEMARY: Suicide? I think of little else.

ANTHONY: What are you saying? You're not serious?

ROSEMARY: The only thing that stops me is my hand. I think of Daddy and what he would want and my hand goes dead on my wrist. Otherwise, I'd be undone by now in a blast.

ANTHONY: What do you mean? What blast?

ROSEMARY: The shotgun.

ANTHONY: Your father's old cannon? You still have it? You're not serious?

ROSEMARY: I am. I keep it behind the door there.

ANTHONY: The ten gauge? But why?

ROSEMARY: Against the depression.

ANTHONY: You're depressed?

ROSEMARY: Are you serious? I'm shattered with depression. I'm shattered with black clouds of depression.

ANTHONY: No. But why?

ROSEMARY: Since I quit the cigarettes.

ANTHONY: Oh yeah. I heard you'd shaken off the damn smokes. Very good.

ROSEMARY: No, it isn't. I've thought of taking poison. I can't stand being alive. You can't know it. It's a madness. It's like a kettle boiling blood that comes up into me head from down below. You know. Feelings!

ANTHONY: Jesus. Your own blood turning against you. I can see it.

ROSEMARY: It's like a horror movie. It's only the rare sign from Heaven that gives me hope.

ANTHONY: It's anxiety. That's what it is.

ROSEMARY: Is that the name for it?

ANTHONY: Sure, I have the same thing. Comes over me in waves. It's nothing.

ROSEMARY: But you don't smoke.

ANTHONY: I don't, but maybe I should take it up. I'd be better off, with the anxiety eating me alive as it does.

ROSEMARY: It's feelings boiling up, isn't it?

ANTHONY: Sure I hate them! Feelings are useless.

ROSEMARY: It's worse in a man. I can't stand a man with feelings.

ANTHONY: A man with feelings should be put down.

ROSEMARY: You're right.

ANTHONY: The problem is there's just not enough air in the world to suit me and there never has been. That's all. Modernization has run roughshod over the spaces between things. The stars are suffocating in the sky and the dirt is choking on itself.

ROSEMARY: And you roaming the land with your gizmo, what's that but modern madness?

ANTHONY: 'Tis true.

ROSEMARY: First time I saw you with that outfit was the week after Mam's funeral. I was awful low. I was looking out the window, thinking, What now? And I saw you at the white hedge, swinging that stick like you were teaching the grass to grow. Why'd you take it up?

ANTHONY: Tony's not alive to stop me, and it keeps me from thinking.

ROSEMARY: Then I should get one. Thinking's worse than February.

ANTHONY: The Guinness is good.

ROSEMARY: Do you like it?

ANTHONY: Perfect.

ROSEMARY: It's not the pub.

ANTHONY: No, it's not the pub. But neither do you have to drive down to the pub and face the garda on the way home.

ROSEMARY: It's terrible the way the garda persecute the country folk with the stops.

ANTHONY: Well, we were murdering ourselves with the automobiles on the black turns of the road. Did you read the story about the six college boys last week?

ROSEMARY: I read it.

ANTHONY: They were going a hundred on a lane as wide as my leg. Spattered themselves across the road. There was a badger licking the blood when the bodies were found.

ROSEMARY: I'll think of that detail as I drift off tonight.

ANTHONY: Don't.

ROSEMARY: I will. Imagine their mothers.

ANTHONY: I won't do it. It's too awful.

ROSEMARY: You should come by more. A girl needs a chat.

ANTHONY: Sure, and a man does, too. Rosemary. I have news.

ROSEMARY: I knew it.

ANTHONY: You did not.

ROSEMARY: I knew there must be something to get you within sight of the house.

ANTHONY: It's true. My cousin is coming from America.

ROSEMARY: Who?

ANTHONY: Frank's son. Adam Reilly.

ROSEMARY: Adam. Imagine naming your child after the first man on earth.

ANTHONY: I suppose they did. He's going to want to be brought 'round.

ROSEMARY: They must've had the Bible open to the first page.

ANTHONY: I suppose so.

ROSEMARY: What do you mean? Brought 'round?

ANTHONY: He's going to want to meet people.

ROSEMARY: Which?

ANTHONY: You'd be good.

ROSEMARY: Me?

ANTHONY: Why not?

ROSEMARY: Why?

ANTHONY: If you want to know the utter truth, I believe Adam is coming from America in search of a wife.

ROSEMARY: A wife.

ANTHONY: He has an idea that an Irish woman would be made of better stuff then these girls he meets in America.

ROSEMARY: There's truth in that. And you want me to help him find somebody.

ANTHONY: You could do that I suppose.

ROSEMARY: How about Mary O'Connor?

ANTHONY: Mary O'Connor!? Does she still have that whistling tooth?

ROSEMARY: She does.

ANTHONY: And ankles like shackles spilling out of her shoes?

ROSEMARY: Hard worker though. She can rip an aluminum can with her hands.

ANTHONY: God love her. I was thinking more somebody like you.

ROSEMARY: Me what? Who's like me?

ANTHONY: Well, you are. I was thinking you might let him take a look at you.

ROSEMARY: Take a look at me in what way?

ANTHONY: Your beauty.

ROSEMARY: My beauty?

ANTHONY: Yes.

ROSEMARY: This is the first I've heard of it.

ANTHONY: Don't pretend you don't know you're beautiful. Half of Mullingar has been to your door.

ROSEMARY: Tony Reilly, you've lived a rock's throw since the day of me birth and this is the first I've heard about beauty.

ANTHONY: Are you going to denounce me for bringing it up?

ROSEMARY: And you want to what, put me in the shop window? Like one of those Euro floozies in Amsterdam?!

ANTHONY: What the hell are you talking about Amsterdam?

ROSEMARY: Amsterdam! You know what I'm talking about! Naked women on parade in the windows of Amsterdam!

ANTHONY: We're talking about my cousin! He's a solid man. He's never even been to Amsterdam I don't think.

ROSEMARY: But you'd bring him here to look me over. Like I was a red heifer.

ANTHONY: I see what you mean about the smoking and giving it up, Rosemary. You're not yourself.

ROSEMARY: How would you know?

ANTHONY: Your temper is rough.

ROSEMARY: Did he offer you money?

ANTHONY: Who?

ROSEMARY: Your cousin.

ANTHONY: For what?

ROSEMARY: Why would you go out of your way like this? You know what it is? There's a name for it. It's human trafficking.

ANTHONY: Human trafficking? It is not!

ROSEMARY: It's all over the news. You heard me.

ANTHONY: He's my cousin. He's a fine lad. And he's lonely.

ROSEMARY: Half the world is lonely and you wouldn't knock on my door about that. Look out the window at the rain and the gloom and the empty land and tell me why that hasn't made you knock on my door, if loneliness made people knock on doors. What is it about this Adam—that he's named after the original man is still strange to me. Why for Adam do you knock?

ANTHONY: I don't know.

ROSEMARY: WHY NOT FOR YOURSELF?!

ANTHONY: What's that?

ROSEMARY: Why not for yourself? If you found me beautiful and lived a hen's kick away from the day I began, why have you not for yourself knocked on the door?

ANTHONY: Maybe I should come back another time?

ROSEMARY: Now don't make me reach out from behind the door the shotgun. 'Cause I will.

(He jumps up.)

ANTHONY: Jesus, Rosemary for the love of God, if it's this bad, go back on the cigarettes. There's cures for cancer easier than your mood.

ROSEMARY: Oh, you'd put me back on the smokes, would ya? Bad cess to yuh.

ANTHONY: Don't be cursing me!

ROSEMARY: After what I've been through. Sit down again.

ANTHONY: I won't sit.

ROSEMARY: You will.

ANTHONY: Calm down then.

(He sits.)

ROSEMARY: Drink your Guinness.

(He does.)

Are you a homosexual?

(He jumps up again.)

ANTHONY: What? What's happened to your mind?

ROSEMARY: Are you gay? Are you gay?

ANTHONY: No.

ROSEMARY: Sit.

(He sits.)

Are you disabled?

ANTHONY: No.

ROSEMARY: A morphodite?

ANTHONY: What the hell is a morphodite?

ROSEMARY: I don't know. Are you oddly put together somehow? Do you have something extra?

ANTHONY: Will you remember that you'll see me at church?

ROSEMARY: I thought you might find me ugly and there's no answer to that, but when you go and give out that you find me beautiful, and that you're not after the boys, well then why, in the name of Cinderella's shoe, would you try to give me away to a cousin you barely know?

ANTHONY: It's a solid idea.

ROSEMARY: Foisting a stranger on me? Are you a pimp?

ANTHONY: A pimp? No, I'm not a pimp. He's a cousin. He's a fine lad. He's an earner. And he stands the same height as you.

ROSEMARY: What kind of badge is that? A woman doesn't want the same height in a man. A man the same height as a woman is short.

ANTHONY: What are you talking about? Are you short?

ROSEMARY: No.

ANTHONY: Then a man the same height is not short.

ROSEMARY: He is.

ANTHONY: That makes no sense.

ROSEMARY: You stand taller.

ANTHONY: Why should you look up at me when you could look straight ahead at him?

ROSEMARY: Because men are beasts and need height to balance the truth and goodness of women.

ANTHONY: There's no answer to blather like that.

ROSEMARY: Then don't answer. You should have come for yourself, Tony. You stand on the same land I do!

ANTHONY: Which is another thing. We're neighbors.

ROSEMARY: That should be a plus.

ANTHONY: It's not.

ROSEMARY: It is. It is. I had reason to think you'd make a move, but nothing came of it. I thought maybe it was the cigarettes put you off so I quit at last.

ANTHONY: You did that with regards to me?

ROSEMARY: I did. And it brought me to my knees I can tell you. I only smoked so that I wouldn't feel while I waited. Now look at me! My eyes could set fire to Gomorrah! My emotions are unspeakable, Anthony, unspeakable.

ANTHONY: But I never said a word about the smokes.

ROSEMARY: You did. You spoke against them.

ANTHONY: I didn't mean it.

ROSEMARY: What do you mean? I have no gift for reading your mind, Anthony, though I've tried. When all seemed lost, I prayed for a sign, and sure I got one as strong as a kick. Still you never came for me and the years passed.

ANTHONY: You got a sign?

ROSEMARY: As plain as grace.

ANTHONY: The white heather?

ROSEMARY: No.

ANTHONY: What was it?

ROSEMARY: What does it matter if you didn't come?

ANTHONY: Well, I've had signs, too, that told me the reverse.

ROSEMARY: What?

ANTHONY: I should have never come today.

ROSEMARY: Is it Fiona? Are you still mooning over Fiona?

ANTHONY: To hell with Fiona. I opened my heart to her and she ran like the wind. That's all there was to that.

ROSEMARY: What did you say to her?

ANTHONY: Never mind that.

ROSEMARY: So there's the secret. Are you in love with another other than Fiona?

ANTHONY: Stop the cross-exam.

ROSEMARY: Are you without feelings in general?

ANTHONY: I have feelings. Though I'd rather not.

ROSEMARY: Do you have any feelings towards me? Or am I alone with this? *(He doesn't answer)* Have you ever wondered what I wore when I wore less?

ANTHONY: You've lost me.

ROSEMARY: Have you stripped me off down to the skin in your imagination?

ANTHONY: Jesus Christ, Rosemary! Shut up with that. I see you at church.

ROSEMARY: You say I'm beautiful. Have you thought about my beauty? Have you dwelt on my beauty, my face, my form, my shape?

ANTHONY: I don't know.

ROSEMARY: Do you know that I have a shape?

ANTHONY: I suppose.

ROSEMARY: You know I'm a woman, and that I have parts that are swollen up and exaggerated to attract the man . . .

ANTHONY *(Overlapping)*: Shut up!

ROSEMARY *(Overlapping)*: . . . to make a man look where he's not supposed to look.

ANTHONY: I refuse to know what you're talking about!

ROSEMARY: Do you know I have a shape?

ANTHONY: Yes, I know you have a shape!

ROSEMARY: Thank God for that.

ANTHONY: Sure I was raised on a farm and seen it all.

ROSEMARY: As have I. But you don't act it.

ANTHONY: How would I act? What would I do? Have my tongue swinging around?

ROSEMARY: There's a good distance between winking and drooling.

ANTHONY: Let's leave it that I know the facts.

ROSEMARY: The facts.

ANTHONY: I've seen it all.

ROSEMARY: Sure you're a master at the game. It's one thing to look at the horses and another to look at your own breed at work. Wait.

ANTHONY: What?

ROSEMARY: Are you a virgin? Is that it? Were you going to give me away to this cousin Adam out of ignorance of yourself?

ANTHONY: What's come over you, Rosemary? You've been chaste as a dove all me life. Now of a sudden you're going on like a pirate! I would never have started in talking about anything if I knew we'd end up talking about everything. I've always thought you were pretty. I didn't think it right to say. That's all.

ROSEMARY: Why not?

ANTHONY: Because one thing leads to another, and we live on top of each other. *(Blushes)* I mean, I mean, close by.

ROSEMARY: Well, what's wrong with one thing leading to another?

ANTHONY: We already live on a patch, it's like sharing half a coffin. If anything went wrong, God's mercy on us! I can hear your kettle whistle when I'm in the shed. We'd be throwing daggers over the fence.

ROSEMARY: You can't live AGAINST life, Tony. You can't avoid harm by avoiding good. What? Would you spend your life swinging your electric detector over the land looking for loose buttons in the rain? Do you not want love?

ANTHONY: What about you, Rose?

ROSEMARY: What about me?

ANTHONY: You've turned down a dozen men over the years! You're notorious.

ROSEMARY: For what?

ANTHONY: Nothing. You're notorious for nothing. For wasting your life and your great beauty, smoking and moping and mopping your way to old age.

ROSEMARY: Well, I quit smoking, and I'm damn well near the end of my mopping and moping. And there you are. You've done it again.

ANTHONY: What have I done?

ROSEMARY: Called me beautiful. And stopped there like a stone. Don't you understand? You're the reason I look at the shotgun.

ANTHONY: Me? What did I do?

ROSEMARY: Why did you knock for an American man and not for yourself?

ANTHONY: There's reason.

ROSEMARY: Look at my face and tell me.

ANTHONY: I told Fiona and she ran for her life.

ROSEMARY: I'm not Fiona. Tell me.

ANTHONY: Don't. I'm cracked. I'm mad. Leave it at that.

ROSEMARY: You're mad?

ANTHONY: I am genuinely off-kilter.

ROSEMARY: Because you hate people?

ANTHONY: No I don't. I have the Kelly madness. Don't make me say it. Me own mam said don't say.

ROSEMARY: And yet you will say. I've sat here in this house for more years than my grandmother LIVED, waiting for you to notice my heart lighting up the way down the old boreen to you. Tell me why you haven't come.

ANTHONY: I did come.

ROSEMARY: Never. When?

ANTHONY: Three years ago. But I turned back. Right there at the white hedge.

ROSEMARY: Why?

ANTHONY: Because I'm cracked. I'm mad.

ROSEMARY: Why are you cracked? How are you cracked?

ANTHONY: You want to know everything? Alright. Here it is. I believe that I am a honeybee.

ROSEMARY: Say that again.

ANTHONY: I believe that I am a honeybee.

(Pause.)

ROSEMARY: But you live in a house, not a hive.

ANTHONY: I think of it as a hive.

ROSEMARY: You can't fly.

ANTHONY: I believe I can fly.

ROSEMARY: How long have you thought you were a bee?

ANTHONY: Enough of me life that you might as well say all of it.

ROSEMARY: This is what you told Fiona?

ANTHONY: That's what I told her and she ran like Satan.

ROSEMARY: And this is why you've never told me I was beautiful?

ANTHONY: That, and the nearness of your farm to mine. And it's true, bees don't like smoke.

ROSEMARY: Well, I'm fed up.

ANTHONY: With what?

ROSEMARY: All that stands in the way. I don't care if you think you're a bee, Anthony. I don't care if you ARE a bee. I'm half dying with living for you. But wait, do you think I'm a bee?

ANTHONY: No.

ROSEMARY: You don't?

ANTHONY: You are NOT a bee.

ROSEMARY: I'm not?

ANTHONY: No.

ROSEMARY: May I know what I am?

ANTHONY: You're a flower. The most beautiful bloom that grows.

ROSEMARY: Oh. Oh. Do you really think that of me?

ANTHONY: Yes and more. And each time a fella came to try his luck with you, I suffered like Christ himself.

ROSEMARY: Oh Anthony.

ANTHONY: But I wish you had married one of those men, my dearest, to end my torture, because I'm no good for nothing and no one.

ROSEMARY: You're good for me. You knocked me down in the yellow grass when I was six, and it was you from then. I've been cleaning this kitchen till my hands were glass, hoping the day would come you would enter here and sit there. And now that day has come.

ANTHONY: That day has not come. Marry Adam. Go to America.

ROSEMARY: You really want me gone?

ANTHONY: Yes! I had a sign. I came to your door with me mother's ring three years past, but when I reached in the pocket, nothing. It was gone.

ROSEMARY: Is that what you've been doing with that gizmo? Looking for your mother's ring?

ANTHONY: That I lost it was a sign. A man who thinks he's a bee should not marry.

ROSEMARY: Why not?

ANTHONY: Because he's mad.

ROSEMARY: What do bees know of madness? The thing that makes you feel crazy is the very thing that proves you sane. You know you're a man.

ANTHONY: A man who thinks he's a bee.

ROSEMARY: But if you know it's odd that you think you're a bee, are you not sane? And why have you gone on looking for the ring?

ANTHONY: It was my mother's.

ROSEMARY: Bees don't have mothers with rings. Men do. And men bring rings to women why?

ANTHONY: Leave off.

ROSEMARY: What would you have done if you found it?

ANTHONY: When?

ROSEMARY: Ever.

ANTHONY: But I didn't.

ROSEMARY: But if you had?

ANTHONY: Oh, I'd have offered it to you.

ROSEMARY: Give us a chance.

ANTHONY: But I couldn't find the ring.

ROSEMARY: Give us a chance, man.

ANTHONY: If it was meant to be, I'd have found it.

ROSEMARY: WE SAY what's meant, Tony! Life is here! We name it! Be bold for me!

ANTHONY: But I've told Adam about you.

ROSEMARY: Tell him to go the hell to Amsterdam!

ANTHONY: Would you leave off Amsterdam!

ROSEMARY: Tell him I'm yours.

ANTHONY: But you're not.

ROSEMARY: Make me yours.

ANTHONY: But I'm mad as a Kelly!

ROSEMARY: I don't care.

ANTHONY: I think I'm a honeybee. I fly around in my mind like a tiny thing.

ROSEMARY: Look at me! Look how I look at you. I have no skin so tender I am to you.

ANTHONY: And I am a virgin.

ROSEMARY: We'll solve that.

ANTHONY: But I think I'm a honeybee! Even now, I'm choking with being in the house. I'm only happy in the fields, or by the window where I can feel the wind and imagine my wings in the free air.

ROSEMARY: You can have the wind and the fields and all the windows up! Here, sure, you fool, here's the ring!

ANTHONY: What's this? You have it?! My mother's ring?

ROSEMARY: I found it by the door three years ago.

ANTHONY: Why didn't you say?

ROSEMARY: I thought it Heaven sent to stop me from suicide and give me hope.

ANTHONY: Three years looking and there it is!

ROSEMARY: I prayed for a sign, and there was my prayer's answer in my hand.

ANTHONY: And the thing that stopped me from knocking.

ROSEMARY: What do I have to do? Do I have to swat at you to get you to sting me? Because I will. You see me as a flower? That's the sweetest thing.

ANTHONY: We should be thinking, Rosemary, not rash. We're neighbors. I see you at church. We'll kill each other when it goes wrong. I should go away out into the air!

ROSEMARY: Think of me as the open door.

ANTHONY: I've never thought of you without fear.

ROSEMARY: Why now fear?

ANTHONY: The pain. Of love.

ROSEMARY: Think of the pleasure. Take your ring.

ANTHONY: Bad luck! Sure it's yours, is it not? It always was.

(He kisses her. It's a good one. They breathe.)

ROSEMARY: I'm mad, too, you know.

ANTHONY: How are you mad?

ROSEMARY: You'll find out. When it's too late.

ANTHONY: Jesus. All those years wasted.

ROSEMARY: Who knows the way things should be? There's beauty in this.

ANTHONY: Will you take down the gates?

ROSEMARY: Never!

ANTHONY: The voice I heard in the fields. It didn't say go. Not just that. It said, "Go to her."

ROSEMARY: Look. The sky.

(They look out a window. The sun is breaking free of the clouds. The sun lights Anthony and Rosemary's faces. "Wild Mountain Thyme" plays.)

END OF PLAY

JOHN PATRICK SHANLEY is the author of numerous plays, including *Doubt: A Parable* (winner of the Pulitzer Prize and Tony Award for Best Play), *Danny and the Deep Blue Sea*, *Beggars in the House of Plenty*, *Dirty Story*, *Where's My Money?*, *Four Dogs and a Bone*, *Defiance* and *Storefront Church*. His sole television outing resulted in an Emmy nomination for *Live from Baghdad* (HBO). In the arena of film, *Moonstruck* garnered him an Academy Award for Best Original Screenplay. Other screenplay credits include *Five Corners*, *Congo*, *Alive* and *We're Back!* Mr. Shanley wrote and directed both *Joe Versus the Volcano* and *Doubt*; the latter earned five Oscar nominations, including Best Adapted Screenplay. In 2008, the Writers Guild of America recognized Mr. Shanley's contribution to film with a Lifetime Achievement Award.

Printed in the USA
CPSIA information can be obtained
at www.ICGtesting.com
JSHW080006150824
68134JS00021B/2316